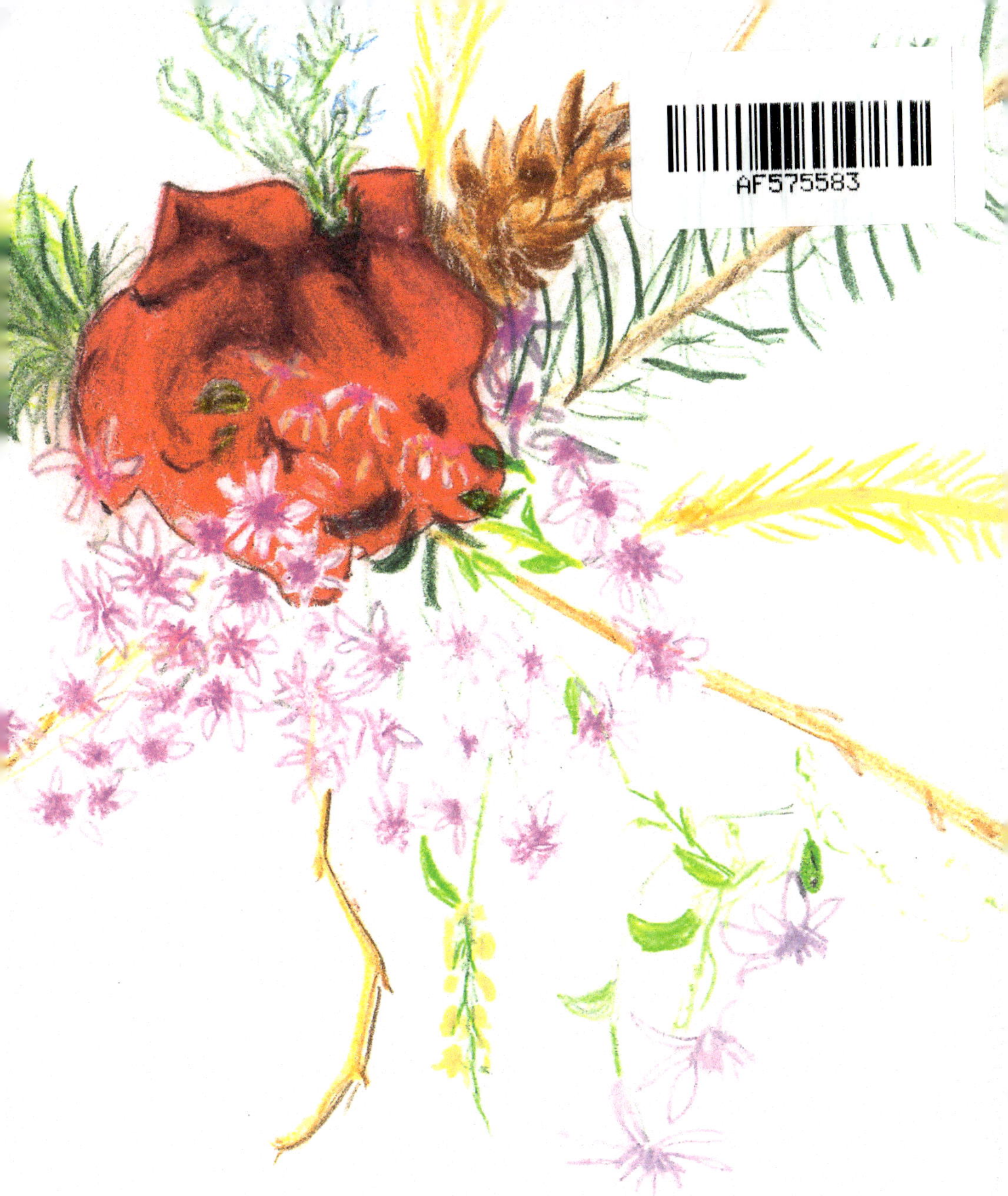

Crowded House

Safia Jama

Crowded House

Safia Jama

www.beltwayeditions.com

Printed in the United States of America
10 9 8 7 6 5 4 3 2 1

Book Design: Jorge Ureta Sandoval
Author Photo: Linda Ibbotson
Cover Art: Sharon C. Peters
ISBN: 978-1-957372-05-1

Beltway Editions (www.beltwayeditions.com)
4810 Mercury Drive
Rockville, MD, 20853
Indran Amirthanayagam: Publisher
Sara Cahill Marron: Publisher

Table of Contents

Part III:
A Doll's House

Safia Jama

****

Crowded House

****

Aubade with Crows

I wake to a throat
full of crows—

thunder and lightning,
followed by a ten-year
drizzle.

The crops don't care
to hear the story.

I left you
my lucky bamboo
on the sill—

in the fridge,
a cup full
of blood.

Part I:

Diasporas

Wedding Day

There should have been roses…
Instead, I clutched red and
white carnations.

We should have invited a few
friends, had a party after,
but such things aren't possible
when one secret marries another.

We got married at 9am
on a Monday morning.

Afterwards, we ate breakfast
at the Happy Days diner
on Montague Street.

My aunt cried as she drove down
from Boston on the I-95
to watch her niece
marry a stranger.

I'm a gambler at heart,
and I slapped my heart down
on the green table.

People I'd known all my life
had let me down, too often.

My father called from...
was it Djibouti? Abu Dhabi?

"Do you two realize what
you're getting into?"

I'm a philosopher at heart:
this was my big moment.

"How could we know?
How does anyone know?"

Diasporas

I grew up in a place called Parkway Village, built for the first employees of the United Nations.

People often want to know, so I'll tell you, yes,
my father worked for the UN.

At the village entrance, a sign still reads:
A Colonial Village of Distinctive Charm.

I have no idea when they put up that sign.

*

Everyone in my immediate family loves Frank McCourt.
At a book signing, my mother told Frank she married
a Somali nomad.

"Must make for interesting pillow talk," said Frank.

My mother says Dad could write the Somali version of
Angela's Ashes, what with all
the hardship he suffered. She says his childhood was *Dickensian.*

*

My father was born to nomadic pastoralists, near
the Somalia-Ethiopian border.

My father does not know his birthday.
I asked, and he said he was born *some summer.*

A British civil servant gave him a fake birthday, Christmas Eve,
making him a year older than he likely was, so he could become
a third grade teacher at age 12.

I've decided he must be a Cancer.
Then again, he might be a Leo.

He remembers lions from his childhood.

*

I once saw a traditional Somali *akal* at the Smithsonian
in Washington, D.C.

In Somaliland we visited our driver's village and I saw his family's *akal*, but there was blue plastic tarp on top of the sticks and animal hide.

Shortly before we left, a hard-of-hearing boy tried to touch my face.
"It's time to go," said Mom.

*

When my father was sick, I became restless. I packed a pink suitcase and went off wandering. I made it to Paris, New Orleans, and Sunset Park.

*

In the early 90s, my cousin Abdi left a refugee camp,
and somehow made it to our home
in Queens, New York. He didn't stay with us long.

My mother took him clothes shopping on Jamaica Avenue.
She kept saying, "He's just a skeleton."

One day, Abdi got lost and disoriented in the subway.
He exited the turnstile, and then re-entered through the gate.

Two men in plain clothes tackled him to the ground.
He fought back, and they beat him up.

He didn't believe their badges.

My father went to get my cousin out of jail.
"He thought they were trying to rob him."

My father was very angry.
I felt a terrible guilt.

Had I left Abdi alone that day, somewhere in the city?

*

In high school, I didn't have the words for what I felt.

I did my homework, joined the track team.
I spent ten hours each Saturday writing my English essay.

750-1000 words on Hamlet, for example.

I was slow, but could tolerate pain.
I ran the 800, badly.

Once I won the bronze medal at Randall's Island.
Curtis, my teammate, cheered me on and afterwards said,
"Nice kick."

I felt good that day in my Champion bicycle shorts.

*

Abdi's mother died when he was young.
His father died in the civil war, making him a true orphan.

*

At some point in his adult life, my grandfather quit being a nomad, and joined the British Merchant Marines.

He visited his family every two years.

"Once, while he was home," said my father, "I remember
my father put his hand on my shoulder."

Fearing that was the end of the story, I began talking incessantly.

*

My Dad's eldest brother used to beat his younger brothers while they were out watering camels in the bush.

"The nomads did that sometimes, for discipline," he said. We sat at the dining table, eating butter cookies.

This was a story I'd never heard before.

Home from boarding school, my father decided that he'd had enough.
He left his younger brother Ali behind, and ran.

He ran many miles across the bush, and the birds offered him directions.
He somehow found his mother.

*

After my grandpa Abdillahi had been at sea awhile,
he had a realization.
His eldest son must attend school and learn English.

He wrote this in a letter to his wife. After the holy man finished reading her the letter, she thought awhile.

I'll need Bashe to help with the camels.

She thought of her youngest son, who was soft,
and clung to his older sister.

My father was a homebody.

They called him "The Center Pole" because he clung to the wooden beam that held up the family's *akhal.*

*

When my father was dying, I bought a little pink suitcase and went off in search of grasses for my goats.

I'm obsessed with tea and scones and, for a long time, I had an English mother-in-law.

The Empire is in my blood, as is the nomad.

*

The first English book my father read and understood was *David Copperfield.*

His school's headmaster was a retired veteran named Badham who drank lots of beer and left the school grounds littered with his glass bottles, which the children collected, washed and used to store water.

I like to imagine my father, curled up on his cot in the mountains, reading:

WHETHER I shall turn out to be the hero of my own life, or whether that station will be held by anybody else, these pages must show.

*

When I was nineteen, I stood in a room of the Shiekh Mountain school while children ran through bombed out schoolrooms.

The landscape was misty, and sunlit.

Photo

I'm wearing a sailor dress.
Outdoors, grass.

I sit in a lawn chair.
Hands folded in my lap.

My hair, a fiery straw,
tints the whole scene
reddish orange.

Everyone wants to love me
in the late afternoon light.

I'm going down in flames, red
as Mother's red hair.

I'm looking off.
Elsewhere.

Hands folded.
Strangely wooden in my lap.

As if someone has arranged them.

Even in the picture,
you can tell.

I'm already long,
long gone.

In the Garment District, 8'o clock, Thursday evening / wanderings

I walk into a store
that sells only buttons.

*

Second hand smoke
all along the side
streets. Certain streets
slurry more than others.

*

I skip the poetry reading.

*

"The garbage smells," you
said. He said.

I say, "Yes, I know."

*

"If is a dangerous word," says
the Emperor of Buttons. We
talk of Rumi.

*

At the Barnes & Noble in
Union Square, I read

The Velveteen Rabbit.

Zombie undertones?

*

In my heart, I know I will never be a vegan.

*

The moon is half-full.
More than that.

*

Aunt Janet turned 70 today.

*

Will I ever smoke again? No,
I don't think so.

*

All the children's books are either
pro-capitalism or nihilistic celebrity crap.

*

Eddies of second hand
smoke all along 38th
street. I pause at
the window of the
button shop.

*

M train. I wait until
the crazed man
is off, and get on.

*

I must change my life.
I must give up cheese.

*

What is a dream and
what is a fantasy?

*

I am troubled by the
Skin Horse.

*

The co-workers sitting across
from me on the train have run
out of small talk. They
watch me write, now that
I have made eye contact.

*

Will I ever drink coffee
again? Will I resist?

*

"It is better to make a mistake
than to do nothing," says
the Emperor of Buttons.

"Do not be afraid
of yourself."

Meditation on Memory

It's strange how things that happened before we were born
get braided into our consciousness—bits and pieces of
stories, passed down, like oddly matched furniture.

My mother, father, and brother, for example, escaping
Somalia is something I never witnessed,
and often forget it ever happened. The way my aunt

Janet wired my mother a lie, that their mother Mary was ill—
and my father, already out of the country, at a conference
on peace in Norway, let's say—or maybe Belgium?

My mother must have had trouble sleeping in the nights
leading up to their escape—and she told no one save
Maryam, the woman who held and hugged my brother

through his baby years. My mother has told me little,
except that they left all the furniture, untouched,
and that she waited all night, holding her baby son

in a steaming Cairo airport, alone, running
from a military dictator who had began to jail friends
and close associates. It wasn't safe. This story, too,

is braided into my childhood injuries, and that of everyone
in my immediate family. So when my husband and I parted
ways, it seemed natural to me to pack, as if, for a day trip,

telling no one save two friends, and my mother was angry.
"Why are you giving up that apartment?" she asked.
I couldn't explain, really. I only knew I had to leave.

G Train. Spattered White Paint. Last Car.

I carry from our apartment 1 blue backpack,
formerly empty, now full of clothes.

Also, a black purse full of miscellania:

—Bacitracin, use by 3/17 (oops)
—eyelash curler in need of cleaning
—*Notes from a Black Woman's Diary* by Kathleen Collins,
of which I've read one chapter—no, two.
—two drugstore nail files intended for my feet
—a Medieval Tarot deck (Scapini) which I purchased at the Met Museum shop
—sunscreen that turns me white
—*Paradise* by Toni Morrison, borrowed from a woman in a nonfiction workshop who said, "Keep it for a whole fuckin' year, I don't mind." that was eight years ago.

—Two loose single dollar bills found in odd pockets as I searched the house for things that I like,
but not so much that they will make me miss my old
life.

Sat. 7:50pm
Sept. 7, 2019.

Biopsy, Washington Heights Location

The 66th Street waiting
room is much nicer,
albeit more impersonal.

"Miss Bower" is called into
the exam room—she's straight
outta *The Bell Jar* with green
sneakers and green eyes.

The other women speak
softly, in Spanish.

The walls are blank—
the nurse pulls
the seafoam green curtain, closed.

Leafy pattern—
Palm fronds? Weed?

Dad smoked weed those last
few months—must've busted
his pride, he who swore never again
after that party in '68, driving high,
scared shitless.

The waiting room at
66th street has an orchid
and a vase of fresh flowers—the gowns
are blue—here,
for some reason, they are pink.

I hate the pink—bubble-gum pink.

Just before the biopsy, I lost
my evil eye—

I've had it nearly
five years—

yet today, taking off
my necklace,
it jumped off
the chain like
a spark—gone!

I nodded. "Okay."

Pocketed my other charm.
Clear quartz.

Earlier this month,
I met a witch
in Eataly—

She asked to share
my table, eyeing my
necklace:

evil eye, clear
quartz—

"Who made it?" she asked.

"I did. I mean, I selected
the pieces at a shop in New Orleans.

I needed something."

"It looks like a battle," she said. "Between the good
and the evil."

"Oh? Is that bad?"

"No, no," she said. "You follow your intuition.
What feels right to you."

Her bottom row of teeth were small and yellow,
but her eyes were clear. She

told me a very long story about a stone that healed
one of her massage – or was it acupuncture?—clients.

Or maybe it was personal training.

She didn't seem like the exercising type, but she knew a lot about what
she called "healing stones." She told me about
those they call "the keeper of the stones." I glanced
at my watch, internally.

My office hours began in ten minutes.
"I need to go, but nice meeting you. Maybe I'll see you again."

"You never know," she said.

Later,
I thought, she's definitely a witch.

But that didn't spook me at all. In that
way, I've changed.

That's why I didn't go looking for that evil eye
in the exam room. I decided it was a sign—time to

let go of that evil eye. But I'll keep the clear
quartz, the same as I used to wear in 1989.
London. New York.

*

Now the evil eye is lodged at the 1 o'clock
spot in my right breast. They found it on the scan,
and mark it with a tiny, titanium chip.

"Like an ice cream sprinkle,"
the nurse said.

Sylvia Plath has gone from the waiting room
and the ladies jack up the volume
on Spanish news.

There is a public health emergency
and here we are, sitting around
in pink gowns.

There is something I am trying to understand
this week—about life, death,
and change.

Friday, March 13th, 2020

Amber

I was trapped
like a fly
in the amber
of abandonment—

How slowly
I lifted myself up
from the bed
each morning.

How can I accuse you?

I'm the one that stumbled into
this—

I'm the one that dove
right into you,
seeking that honeycomb
of home.

*

Now I regard
the air bubbles
rising up like stars—

I offer myself
here—

Hold me up to the
light—
claim to see through me—

My centuries-old
hurt relegated
to a key chain—

I lock my mouth
up – again and
again—

I lift myself up
from the bed.

The air bubbles may
fool me into
thinking I'm a fish—

I swear you have changed
my brain with your fishes.

Each time you go away,
I keep them alive.

Perhaps I'm not a fish
nor a fly—

but the amber itself.

*

That next year I
met a friend
at summer camp—

Her name was Amber—

I had never befriended
a black girl
at camp before –

Four summers in a
row, I went to camp.

Then one year,
inexplicably,
I told my parents
I don't want to
go.

I didn't want to
see my friends,
or Molly the dog,
or the lake.

I stood in the master bedroom
of our garden home
and said,

"I want to go to Disneyland."

We three drove up the coast from LA
to San Francisco.

My brother, finally gone,
off to college, the Mid-West, etc.

How could I outrun
adolescence?

Like Lolita?

Like Gregor Samsa's kid sister,
finally free and picnicking with her parents
in the sunshine?

I held my breath and dove
under the wave—

and when I resurfaced,
we were stuck in LA traffic.

They had to pull over so I could vomit.

I was always getting carsick.

To this day, I distrust cars,
I don't want one.

*

Iconic photo: my father
and I on the Dumbo ride,
his face a grimace.

Here's a man who
has seen elephants
in the bush—

Elephants, somehow
seem important here.

*

Recently, I cross examined my mother:

"Isn't it strange that I didn't want to go to camp?"

"You had started your period," she said.

*

Maybe this is all I wanted:
to commune with Dad, and Dumbo.

To grab my childhood by the tail

in a formal ritual,
placing a period at the end.

To sit in a flying elephant with my father,
who irritated my mom to no end
announcing that he quit smoking
just as our trip began.

In the photo, my ponytail is flying
in the wind. I wrote that my father
is "grimacing," but actually,
he's smiling.

Would you believe me if I said
we made the evening news?

A special on *Le Quatorze Julliet* holiday.

The TV journalist asked my parents,
"When was the last time you were in Paris?"

Mom and Dad both answered, but I was silent,
having never been.

When we returned home to New York, my mother wrote one of her articles
she sometimes published, locally.

It's Never Too Late to Go to Disneyland.

Remembering Our Birds

I watch sunrise on square windows
that remind me of those reflective aviator glasses
people sometimes wear—

I bought a pair that first spring you visited me,
and I wore them without irony,
just as I used to wear everything.

I left my wardrobe at our old apartment
you kept like a museum, not moving a single
pillow for a year. Your main design contribution,

two Australian zebra finches, purchased that April,
our first big rumble. I left, and you replaced my absence
with caged birds. When I returned in the fall, I learned

to accept our new pets, the vestige of my leaving, the symbol
of our ongoing troubles. When we fought, the birds fought.

When we loved, the birds preened and on the afternoon
I packed to go to my mother's, you picked a newly
hatched chick off the kitchen floor and placed it
in the palm of my hand.

You have to keep it warm or it will die!
My heart had fled the coup, I didn't care,
only I didn't want that warmth to leave,
and we named the chick Baby.

I went to my mother's a week, and Baby grew bigger,
and the parents raised Baby until she became full grown
and belligerent. I had no idea what it meant to save a life

that would eventually turn around and attack,
but then again, I'm not a parent.

This morning, I watched the sunrise across the windows
where I have been a nesting here these nine days.

Olive, the finch that I chose from the pet store, died last year.
You said when you looked into her eyes, she looked back
and called in tears when Olive was ill. You took that $15
bird to the vet and spent $400. She didn't make it,
but I was glad you tried, and so were you.

That's when you found Emily, the small white bird
meant to replace Olive. Pip never took to Emily, though,
so you kept her in a studio apartment nearby and you told me
she enjoys her solitude and spends her time
contemplating poetry.

Last Thanksgiving, our second year apart,
you were out all night, and when you came home,
Emily had drowned herself in the fish tank,
her white feathers bobbing among the Amazon weeds,
Sir Claude, your prized fish, looking on perplexed.

I said it was a very literary death, and felt disturbed and sorry
and fascinated. We were out walking in the snow and you
were trying hard to be kind.

I felt something new,
something akin to the frozen snow—
the winter sun burning the bare trees
touched a pain I needed to feel, to know
that I am still here and alive.

Those first birds, the vestiges of our troubles,
we buried tenderly, side by side,
in Flushing Park beneath a weeping cherry
not far from where I was born.

LaGuardia Plaza Hotel
January 13, 2021

Heather

for Lucie Brock-Broido

Soft squares of pain
  wall paper the desert sands.

Winnowing is a word I
  rarely use, wishing it
   weren't so.

However, however. Heather is
 also a girl's name.

Not a woman, but a
  girl, with feathery
  hair.

Soft, soft is a pause
  in Elizabethan.

Soft. And then antlers,
  bleeding from the inside.

  Leaning
gentle against the snow.

Why I Ate Your Donut (2017)

Cashmere stars broke my heart
every time I tried them on

in the dressing room and the sweater
instantly melted like melted cheese—

to wear it would be too revealing,
like nude glitter on a figure skater.

Come morning, I found your glazed donut
half-smashed in ancient Tupperware:

oatmeal-colored, stained glass.
No allegory, only yellow-red sprinkles

plus a cartoon bite taken from it
as if it were an apple.

Old Photos: London / Lake District

1.

London, Savile Row
… E & Ravense…
Wig shop

I'm wearing my
fuchsia and teal ski
jacket, Gap jeans
with a tapered leg—

My eyes, staring straight
into the camera –

A kind of smile –
as I pose with
the cascading
white blonde
curls – so far
from Brooklyn—

Our Londoner,
Anita, still alive,
smiles unabashedly,
fully in on the joke—
a woman in love
with her life—
black wool coat,
gold hoops,
two black daughters,
and I like

another daughter
to her—

My reflection is
there among the wigs
of power,
intruding,
smiling harder
there, my eyes
closed in that
farther second—
my nails painted
red, I'm leaning
into that
window, one
foot forward like a
Nefertiti—

2.

Dogs Fouling
Footways
and Grass
Verges—

South Lakeland
District Council

My mother has
photographed a
sign warning,

"It is an offense under a bylaw in operation throughout
the district for a person in charge of a dog

to allow the dog to foul the footway of any
highway and certain adjoining grass
verges or footways of any public
place by depositing its excrement
thereon.

A.F. Winstanley
Clerk & Chief
Executive"

3.

My mother,
wearing a trench
and white
sneakers, stands
beside an ancient
stone wall—

A chink in the
wall: Beyond that,
a Lake. Faded hills.

Part II:

My Small Room

Moths!

"In forty years, I have never seen
these flies," says Mel.

I say, "They're moths."

"Are you sure?"

"Yes. They're small,
but they *are* moths."

Gloria says, "I cannot be
near those animals!"

Today is Gloria's birthday.
Autumn equinox. I
go into my room.

I can't find my new Joan
Didion reading glasses.

They were to be my last
extravagance before
the long season
of economy.

I suspect the moths are my fault.

That packet of napkins
I bought from
the bad luck grocery
store. A tear in the plastic,
I ignored.

I will never shop there again.

My Small Room

Heart palpitations and a three-day weekend
lies ahead like open sea.

Here's me in a dinghy
tattooed purple:

Le Divorce.

*

Lucinda the Landlord
says her sister stayed in this room for *years
and years…*

Her sister, now in the New Jersey suburbs,
still remembers, *My small room, my small room!*

Now my small room.

My small room, my small room!
is tall enough for a giant.

Such high ceilings!
Such a very tall door!

I keep it empty,
afraid to ruin the effect.

One large, old-fashioned
window with French shutters
that bend every which way,
thick with paint,
but all the hinges work: they fold up
neat as ironed sheets.

I open and close the shutters
each and every day
just for fun.

Two Pin Oaks form a green leafy scene.

I didn't know they were Pin Oaks until this week,
when I saw some at the Botanic Garden,
which, by the way, I can walk to.

It takes hours, but still, I can walk there.

My small room, my small room!
is across the street from the hospital.

Yesterday I noticed pink roses
up in a window.

I imagined I was in the hospital.
I imagined the roses were for me.

I am a convalescent romantic, reclining and exhaling
the fumes of some tea roses I saw
at the Garden last Thursday.

One sign said that Theodore Roosevelt liked a tea rose
for his lapel. Such extravagance!

I'm like the lovesick Duke in Twelfth Night,
who sighs, "If music be the food of love, play on"!

I wear ear buds and lie on my stomach,
gazing out the window:
I call it windowing,
watching *Birds on a Branch*
and other hit shows on the cat TV.

My hands hold the pillow
like a stuntman hanging from a ledge.

I eat raw almonds, replenishing iron,
all the blood I've lost
these last few years
from all the sword cards
plaguing every Tarot spread.

Ten for my father.
Three for my heart.

Seven swords made this borrowed bed,
rescued from some fleeing tenant
who left behind ten strands
of long, black hair.

Lucinda's husband, Mel, finds the mattress and frame
in the basement: mostly clean, largely intact.

I deem it "Just right."

A Goldilocks bed
for my Goldilocks room,
far from the kitchen
where people will talk.

Cue Roomie Gloria's side-eye:

They didn't tell me about that bed
when I took the small room.

I smile sweetly, and say,
"I can be very charming,"
(which, I realize, isn't
a very charming thing to say).

But I feel I have to explain this blip,
this trick of luck.

This feast or famine
that has followed me through the years,
making me appear
melodramatic or lucky or brave,
it's always all or nothing with me.

I can still hear my mother saying,
"Don't be such a martyr!"
that one time I expressed my feelings,
aged sixteen.

"I'm feeling overwhelmed," I'd said.
I never said it again.

Alas, you can't luck your way
through a marriage. At some point,
the car won't start.

Like I said, all or nothing.
That's that.

So I cling to the ledge and listen
to Luke Kelley sing Raglan Road,
the song Vincent sang to me
in Carna while I sat palely
recovering from a bad
oyster. Behind him
out the window I saw rainbows
and woods and actual, real
pheasants. (Vincent had seen one
out walking, alone.)

As he sang, I remembered the young
woman who wanted more
than anything to be
an artist, like him.

I would have stayed forever,
if only for the music. A child to his
Pied Piper.

I'd stay on for the Foggy Mountain
Breakdown. Live banjo,
as I washed the dishes
in a deep trance.

His Concertina would heave
airs as I sipped tea. Not a bad
way to spend a life,
and yet, nothing I ever did
seemed all that important
or so interesting
with so much music
filling my ears.

I became spacious
as a river
without water.

Like Joni tells it:

> *I love you when*
> *I forget about me*

*

My small room is too bare. I am depriving myself
of anything that feels like a home.

I need to fill it up a bit more.
I need to admit that this is my real life.
This is not pretend.

Gloria works in the showroom
at Restoration Hardware. Rich people,
Meat-Packing district. She speaks
to me in the tones of a doctor
as she says:

It's very simple.
You need to spend two-hundred and fifty dollars at Ikea.

Her first language is Spanish, and I agree with her coworker,
who told her, "Gloria when you speak, I feel like dancing!"

Right now, though, I don't feel like dancing.

I nod solemnly, recalling how a month ago,
I'd been too stubborn to face Ikea.

Instead, I spent $55 on an "organic mineral" pedicure
and then I bought a French teapot for another 50.

I laundered Gloria's old duvet and bought
white hospital sheets at Target.

I like weird combinations of extravagance
and asceticism. I boil water in my French
teapot named *Marine.*

I'm a soldier at sea.

I keep French perfume
on the table just like I said I would
in that long-ass poem
I read in D.C. After I read,
the curator had said,

"Everyone, as a reminder please keep to your five minute limit…"

Afterwards a young Leonard Cohen look-alike
approached and said,

Yours is the first voice I've heard in a long time
that I want to spend time with.

I immediately fell in love with him.
I found out his name and then stalked him online for weeks.

*

Flashback to house-sitting.
That week between apartments.

I bought a side table
from a man in Bed-Stuy.

A charmer, he slowly shook
the palm of a passerby

Before accepting my tenner
and two singles.

His smooth choreography prompted me say,
"You're here every Sunday?"

"Seven days a week!" he smiled.
Full wattage, so bright,
I had to blink twice.

*

Sometimes I think I suffer
from a surplus of some sort.

Or as Duke Orsino would say,
A surfeit.

I used to love my stuffed animals
so damn hard, I swear,
they loved me back.

They raised families and lived full lives.

*

Strange, to live so close to a hospital.

Lucinda worked the late shift
for thirty years.

She tried to teach me the meaning
of "diversion," a hospital term
involving ambulances.

I guess the ER is like a nightclub.
You need to be on the list
to get in.

"They used to line up, all night,"
says Lucinda, "and then my supervisor said,
'No diversions!' So I had to turn them away…"

She sighs, and I still can't tell from context
what diversion means and Lucinda can't
hear me. She's got hearing loss.

Sometimes, she looks at me
in a way I can't describe.
It's terrible. At first I was offended,
but I think it's just the look
of a person being erased
from a conversation.

Week two.
Lucinda lets herself into our apartment
during a downpour to check the windows
in the still-vacant room.

I am sitting in the kitchen
in my nightgown.

She is faraway, or I am faraway,
so I can't quite scold her for breaking in.

I am, after all, living in her house.

Some day I will miss all this,
and chant, like Lucinda's sister,

My small room, my small room!

How We Met

I started as a fan,
two eyes

twinkling in the dark, salty dribbles
down to my lips—

a lifeline on my cheek.

I didn't want you yet in that Galway garden of cigarettes and swans. We drank cans by the bay, lit by the moon, candy colored houses all subdued. Our laughter, the sleeping swans… I dropped my pill on the floor of The Vic. *I can't find it.* I said. *I can't see the floor!* You found it for me in the dark.

The first night, Joe asked to put his hand
Just there. Would you mind? he asked.

I didn't. I saw it, his golden opportunity—
my perfect stomach with one tiny suture.

He closed his eyes, and sighed
as if I were the high, holy grail.

The sun rose, I was his daffodil.
And you, glowering.

Morning. Your man's breakfast, poached eggs
on butter toast balanced on the knees
of a space heater.

Our love, a one room hovel-cum-home.

I fell for your address, itself a poem.

14 Ashley Grove
Knocknacarra
EIRE

Brooklyn, again. I sulk, bait the lines.

Read a book about how to be mean, how to allure him
in a stretchy thong *For beginners*

said the woman at La Petite Coquette.

You could be model said a Russian woman
surveying my legs   stirring the hot wax.

*

I waited for you, my star at the gate.

5:53 am

I wake to Mel's
cigarette smoke
and loud clanging of con-
struction. A healing sleep.
"I felt you," said Gloria,
the Venezuelan
girl in the room next
to me.

We are all grown
women but she says,
"We are just four girls."

I've been alone
for years, so why
should I feel lonely
now? To appease my
therapist's take on
reality and human
emotion? Yet to feel it.
That's a different story.

In my dream a woman
wore shaded glasses
in a deep rose—
I awoke refreshed.

Off-stage healing is my
favorite kind—
dream workers kneading
my veins like bread
dough—delicious

meal come morning,
hot and ready to eat.

Prepared with love
by someone else.

Friday, Sept. 13, 2019

Crying

This morning,
my crying was like
a cracked honey-
comb:
        still warm.

Crying,
like caramel
center
of a chocolate

imported from
deep within.

Crying, like a bottle
of tears, fermenting
since 1983.

This crying,
not *like*,

but actual
remedy.

Roomie

Heavy, wet hair.
Her T-shirt drenched-
out each shoulder.

She carries
a clear, plastic
basin from her room.
Toilet flush.

Next, workmen
arrive to piece
together her bed.

I eat my oatmeal
in a cold sweat
carried to my room,
then back out
again. I can't
think of people
any other way now.

They're not people.
They're characters,

And they are
mine. So I love
this strange girl,
always trailing her
mother's hopes.
Her nausea sends
me into fits of
gratitude. All

the things she
knows that I don't.

That I now do,
or will.

Part III:

A Doll's House

The Puzzle

I found the puzzle inside
a Christmas Cracker,
my last Christmas
in Ireland.

2016. George Michael had
just died.

My dad was sick,
and I quietly stewed
about missing what I knew
would be *his* last Christmas.

The British Isles papers gushed
and fawned over George Michael
after decades of shit talking.
His photos and quotes filled
every paper. He was my girlhood
hero, too, so I lapped
it all up. Cried my crocodile
tears.

After dinner, I cleaned up
on Christmas Crackers.
I pulled and pulled
until the cracker broke.

I won the gifts inside:
vanilla lip balm and a
tiny key chain with
a puzzle attached.

Funny, I forgot
it was a key chain.

I pulled one piece out
after the others had
tried. I succeeded!
Soon the perfect cube
was a neat pile
of pieces scattered
about the table.

I announced that I would
put the puzzle back together,
stretching my fingers
dramatically. My
mum-in-law joked,
"You can't leave the
table till you've finished,
you know."

I shivered a little shiver,
and laughed nervously.

Everyone disappeared
noiselessly to watch
George Michael elegies
on the telly.

Away I went to
work. I sat there
for an hour that
night. Some pieces
slid together nicely,
others vexed me

with irregular
rectangles and
negative spaces I
couldn't visualize.

The puzzle became
a virus in my mind.

I retreated to the granny
flat where we always
stayed. A private
space,
but the toilet
didn't flush
right.

I thought, "After
a nice hot bath,
surely I will
solve the puzzle!"

Hours later, I
felt dizzy and
sick. My husband
found me in
the cold room,
my teeth chattering,
my feet numb.
I gathered up the
pieces and brought
them home to
New York.

This evening, I
took the puzzle

out of my purse,
where it has been
waiting. I thought,

"If I put this
puzzle together,
it will mean
something good.

"If I put the
puzzle together,
I will feel so
smart, so good,
so much better
than the
contemptuous
person who designed it."

Then I thought,

"Perhaps it's
not a puzzle at
all. Perhaps it's
a key chain that
I broke."

            I put
my head down
on the table.

Outside it is
dark. I am
running late to
meet a friend.
I haven't eaten

any of the dinner
I carefully
prepared and
wrapped in tin
foil. I
cry out, "This
puzzle is cursed!"
then throw the
pieces in the
garbage, wincing.

I gather
my wallet and
keys.

I hope to still make
the reading, to see
the friend who
expected to see me
there. I know
that throwing the
puzzle away was
the right thing to
do. I have to
accept this small
failure that has
somehow grown / so big.

Strange voices
plague me.
My mind gapes open
like a landfill.
I fear it.

Miracle

I kid you not, this past winter,
I saw Charles Bronson in mold,
a perfect likeness stamped along
the left hand side of the tub that no one
had cleaned for some time—

That was, by all accounts,
a rough winter,

yet here was a tiny bit of relief,
a symbol of… a symbol of what?
I never got that far,
for I was much too surprised,
and perhaps in my sub-
conscious wondering
whether Charles Bronson in mold
could maybe? possibly? Qualify
as a miracle of some sort?

I am a child of the 80s,
surely many a Bronson flick
graced the TV set,
now and then,
while I was crawling around
in my Osh Kosh corduroys,
sneaking handfuls of dirt
and breathing in second
hand smoke—

I know I said it was winter,
but did I mention that it was

Valentine's Day? I was all
alone in the house,
that night, and dreaming
strange dreams
that whole weekend,
and there he was,
looking a lot like
Che Guevara
(it wasn't Che Guevara)

I kid you not, I saw Charles Bronson in mold
last winter, and my point is
never give up—
for you may also look up one day
to see his sexy, vigilante self ready
to bust open the heads of bad guys,
showing no mercy,

and no, I don't approve of such callow
violence, but I do approve of Bronson's
fitted, battered leather jacket
and how his faintly pock-marked
skin eschews artifice,
all of which could
sound superficial,
yet there isn't
and never will be
anything trivial about easing
into a hot bath
and turning your head to see
a finely chiseled, stoical portrait
of Charles Bronson
in hunter green mold,

and as I comfort myself,
today,
after that man
followed me yesterday,

I turn to the memory
from last winter, when I
was still
recovering,
still healing myself from the way,
way inside wound that winds
through earth's core,

all that magma
and rock,
our freighted burdens,
our fardels far away
and unseen,
yet nonetheless real.

A Doll's House

It's a play I taught, in English,
as a young high school teacher.

We watched the film adaptation starring Jane Fonda,
which another teacher lent me on VHS cassette tape,
slightly grainy.

Fonda, a complete anachronism with her
toothy grin and 70s eyeliner, rocking cowgirl skirts and dancing
the Tarantella in the Arctic darkness
by the light of kerosene lamps.

What I want to say here, at this juncture, is how brilliant
Ibsen left the women of the world a challenge: he said a million
things and he said nothing.

Nora slammed the door, leaving Torvald. She left her babies
and her man to figure it out. She didn't ask for alimony,
and she didn't have a plan
but at least she was wise enough to know
what she didn't know.

Now I will list the clues in my own life: Ibsen's proddings,
my own subconscious.

How the week I fell in love, I glimpsed my first fjord,
angular as a slice / of green cake dotted with Irish wildflowers.

How I taught Nella Larsen's *Quicksand* year after year,
daydreaming about
Helga Crane's voyage across the Atlantic,
her brown skin
and her halting Danish, echoes of her mother; finally,

how my husband brought back from his travels a pair of woolen
blue and white
socks adorned with the flag of Norway
just a few mornings
before we parted for good;
and how then I
went to live among strangers, other women adrift;

and finally, how Deb once told a prospective flatmate,
"You'll hear Safia slamming doors."

The New Apartment

I am inconsolable until one night I make
a replica of my small room—

the likeness is striking: high ceilings,
a long, skinny rectangle like a railway car.

I drape candy-colored lights over the mini-shelf
and close the door, just like I did last year,
quarantining too long, too long…

But there is a comfort in small spaces, sometimes.
and the other room is already cluttered, too much,
energy uncertain and haphazard. Leave it.

I feel a welcome peace, now, after a difficult stretch.
Like my life sometimes catches the light just so,
and I can see the potential,
the smooth side of what's rough. So now I touch
that velvet life and feel all that
it's worth.

I want to stop reaching for the cheap
stuff they keep trying to sell me,
like that wine I drank most of last night,
then dumped
the last glass down the drain, realizing it had
served its purpose.

This morning my sinuses
drained suddenly and I could really taste the pow!
in the leftover lasagna.

Miraculously, I had no
hangover, no headache, all I had were these feelings
and fears. And I still have them,
only now,

they are contained. They are held and named,
and I am grateful for this
little dark room,
the coiled silver heater beside
the white pipe—

I am grateful for the twin bed I bought off
Mel and I'm glad my ex- seems happier in his life.

I know I had some part in it, and I also know it's time
to let myself live *for me.*

Crowded House (Don't Dream It's Over)

Nonsensical beauty. All the plates
he broke on accident remember
happier days. Honey, it's over
but let's still dream of the early days.

That first Christmas in Ireland.
That was something. Tinsel walls,
hors d'oeuvres I would someday
make at parties our friends

would come to miss. Reminiscent
of 1966. My parents' dream kitchen.
Pots and pans float and fade. More
plates explode. One, you broke on

purpose, and I now whisper into
the drummer's ear: "Cameras are
rolling. Smile." Near the end,
Darrell filmed in our living room.

Still together, still hanging on,
though oatmeal stood hardening
on the stove. Future rocks we'd
throw at one another. 1986

was a good year, maybe the last
good year for some time. Now
the lead singer is vacuuming
and soon the bassist will play

an organ solo wearing his Matador
jacket. Mix and match like thrift stores

and flea markets and you and me.
Crowded House has not forgotten

a single detail, pouring over photo
albums. A candelabra lights a corner.
I watched this video every night for days—
then weeks, until, at last, I walked across green
grass did greet me.

Groundwater

Yesterday's low point: stewing over other people's joy
as if I'll never get my own. I don't wanna live like that.

This morning's meticulous breakfast: stale Christmas
cookies crumbled over plain yogurt. Voilà, granola.

I weigh the pros and cons of madness. An appealing
means of escape? Or else, I'll just take a walk.

The fields are muddy these days. Patches of grass
so green. Nourished by sunshine, then snow melt.

Last night, I waited for the new moon.
Perhaps the most difficult thing is knowing

what you yourself are and then accepting that
this puzzle can never safely be disassembled.

Let it be. Groundwater is something we all need.
It can't be made, yet it keeps the earth green and fed.

In the dark of the moon, I dreamt frustrating dreams.
Forgetting my favorite flip flops in a hotel bathroom.

Walking across familiar grounds wearing a soiled
bathrobe after I had been so careful to remain clean.

In the wee hours of morning, I experienced a recognition.
A powerful knowing that I possess all that I need.

And then I thought of groundwater,
and then I heard, *Weep for me.*

Snow makes us taller

I said to the young couple,
or young friends out walking a white fluffy Chow.

I stood on a foot bridge overlooking the frozen lake—
half-ice, half-slush.

That was my first good walk in weeks,
maybe a month.

The railing, the guards,
the bridge had
shortened—

"Snow makes us taller," I thought again,
out walking this morning. I walked
into the snowy park,
into mid-life.

Mid-day, I waited where last summer,
the lake was alive—ducks, milling around,
out on dates, or in squadrons.

Now the water was covered up—
I waited.

A woman and her
curious dog appeared.

I take myself on walks the way
other people walk their dogs.

I stare into bushes and sniff leaves.

"She wants to know what you see,"
said the woman.

"What's under that snow?" I said,
and she laughed and they left.

I turned home, guessing nature had slept late.

Then I heard the tap, tap, tap.
Then I heard the cry of the woodpecker.
Then I saw a young raccoon creep out of
a tree to drink from the stream.
Then a blue jay flew, back and forth,
across the scene.

Then a squirrel bounded into the
powder, heroically, face-first.

Then a flock of sparrows peppered
the sky.

Then I saw the ladder-back with a
red cap, tap, tap,
tapping that freezing
tree—my eyes
had to half-imagine
the intricate
design—the zebra stripes
and tailored feathers.

Nature likes an audience,
like anyone. To be welcomed,
and seen.

Nothing demanded
in return.

ACKNOWLEDGMENTS

Thank you to the editors and magazines who first published the following poems:

— "Aubade with Crows," *Poets of Queens* anthology (2020)
— "Wedding Day," *World Literature Today*. (2022) The first line of "Wedding Day" is from Jens Peter Jacobsen, as quoted in Rilke's *Letters to a Young Poet* (Norton).
— "Photo," *TAB Journal* (2021)
— "Biopsy, Washington Heights Location," *The Rumpus* (2022)
— "Groundwater," *Red Door Series Broadside* (2021)
— "Crowded House" and "Remembering Our Birds," *Prairie Schooner* (2023)
— "Heather," "Meditation on Memory," and "Snow makes us taller," *Action, Spectacle* (2023)

Thank you to Mervyn Taylor, Ryan Black, and Massy Tadjedin for being the first readers of this book. Thank you to my publishers, Indran Amirthanayagam and Sara Cahill Marron.

Thank you to Cave Canem, the Rutgers-Newark MFA Program, The African Poetry Book Fund, Poets & Writers, and Baruch College for providing institutional support through the years. Thank you to all my teaching colleagues and students, past and present.

Thank you to my mother, Virginia.

In memory of James A. Shyne, Sr.

Safia Jama

was born to a Somali father and an Irish American mother in Queens, New York. A Cave Canem graduate fellow, she has published poetry in *Ploughshares*, *Boston Review*, *World Literature Today*, *Prairie Schooner*, and *Poem-a-Day*. Her poetry has also been featured on WNYC's *Morning Edition* and CUNY TV's *Shades of US series*. Jama is the author of *Notes on Resilience*, included in the New-Generation African Poets chapbook box set (Akashic Books, 2020). She is a lecturer in the English Department of Baruch College, City University of New York.

Author Photo: **Linda Ibbotson**

Crowded House

PRINTING WAS COMPLETED IN JULY 2023 FOR **Beltway Editions**